SUNRISE AND SUNSETS

by

Janet Ward

Gotham Books

30 N Gould St.
Ste. 20820, Sheridan, WY 82801
https://gothambooksinc.com/

Phone: 1 (307) 464-7800

© 2023 Janet Ward. All rights reserved.

No part of this book may be reproduced, stored in a retrieval system, or transmitted by any means without the written permission of the author.

Published by Gotham Books (March 07, 2023)

ISBN: 979-8-88775-233-4 (sc)
ISBN: 979-8-88775-234-1 (e)
ISBN: 979-8-88775-235-8 (h)

Because of the dynamic nature of the Internet, any web addresses or links contained in this book may have changed since publication and may no longer be valid.

The views expressed in this work are solely those of the author and do not necessarily reflect the views of the publisher, and the publisher hereby disclaims any responsibility for them.

CONTENTS

To Me 2

I Choose 4

Irony Of Life 6

Butterfly Wings 8

Once I Loved 10

Caged 12

Misspoken Words 14

Rivers 16

A Love Song 18

Hurting Words 20

Sunshine And Stars 22

Safe Places 24

Patterns 26

Moments 28

Touching 30

Pretty Packages 32

God's Touch 34

Being Myself 36

Poetry Of Life 38

Crickets 40

Emergence 42

Anticipation 44

Prerequisites 46

Rest	48
Our Authentic Presence	50
Thinking	52
Join Them	54
Straight Ahead	56
Clocks	58
Our Needs	60
Rivers Again	62
Having You	64
Staying Well	66
Who's To Say	68
Moving The Stones	70
Life	72
At First Sight	74
Habits	76
The Ear	78
Speaking	80
Hearts	82
Cells Of The Heart	84
To Journey	86
Obstacles	88

*These writing were written after
the turn of the century and are dedicated
to friends and family that have been
faithful to encourage and support me.
Your love and confidence in me
makes this book possible.*

TO ME

May your footsteps set you upon a Journey of love.
May you wake each day with His Blessings, and sleep each night in His keeping.
And, may you always walk in His tender care.

09/09/2013

Louisiana Lake
September 09, 2013

I CHOOSE

I choose to live by choice, not chance.
be motivated, not manipulated.
To be useful, not used.
I choose to excel, not compete.
I choose self-esteem, not self-pity.
I choose to listen to my inner voice,
Not the random opinions of others.

05/2012

Las Vegas Luxor
May 2012

IRONY OF LIFE

What is this irony of life?
The old man in the street
His bell ringing an invitation
For his wares.
Kids running in the rain
Muddy feet and jeans,
Laughing at the old man
And splashing him as they
Dance by.
Busy people rushing, going
Somewhere, or nowhere.
Faces with no faces
Smiles that mean nothing.
What does all of this mean,
This irony of life?
I took it all in and ponded
it over and over.
All I saw was a void.
And then I saw you!

11/2001

In flight
November 2001

BUTTERFLY WINGS

Lift your head and focus your eyes
Life and love are passing us by
Lets don't miss it.
We will capture it in a butterfly's
Wing and carry it to our safe place.
Tomorrow we will take time to love,
laugh, and play
and we will take our dreams out of
that butterfly's wing
and share it with the world.
They will see how wonderful this fleeing life
is.

08/2010

At Sea
August 2010

ONCE I LOVED

Once I loved but never like this.
I have loved others
I have loved the smell of the sea
I have loved the wind and the sky.
And once I loved.
Once I loved all of Gods beautiful
Things, and I still do.
Once I loved but never like this.
Every time I look at you
I test myself Again for once
I loved.

08/2010

Canada
August 2010

CAGED

Love, as lovely as it is ensnares.
But it is better to be looking out
From behind the bars, caged and
Contented than on the outside
Alone and free.
Only lonely people know freedom.
But notice, tho, the rope I tied
Around your ankle!
No summer seen can steal you
From me!

07/2010

Louisiana Cottonfield
July 2010

MISSPOKEN WORDS

Misspoken words
Or no words spoken at all.
Changing meanings,
Changing hearts.
Leaving out important parts
Can change a lot of things
But it can only change us
If we let it.

08/2010

Las Vegas
August 2010

RIVERS

There are rivers
I will never see
But I fear that upon that final
Stream I might fall.
With that in mind
I will seek
To see all the rivers
And I will take you with me.
There is always the chance each one
Might be that final one.
And, with the reflections on
The water I will linger with you
And ponder.

07/2010

A LOVE SONG

I wanted to write you a love song.
Some words for you to remember.
Some words that would leap from
The pages, crawl up your arm,
and lay against your cheek.
But, I was lazy, I stayed in bed.
Written words can make it seem
Foolish anyway.
I wanted to write you a love song
Telling you how like yourself you are.
Yes, we are what we are.
But before I got the pen to write it down
You were gone, so without you the song
Has no words.

09/2012

Baha California
September 2010

HURTING WORDS

Lies and hurting words tear at
The heart.
No matter where you have been
Or what you have done,
Honesty about your self-worth
Always seem the best to me.
Speak gently to the ones you love
So, they don't turn away and
Rush back into their own mind.

09/2015

Mississippi Sunrise
September 2015

SUNSHINE AND STARS

I fit so well here
The amazing aspens
With leaves glistening
In the sun
It didn't rain today
I wished it had so everyone
Would stay away.
I love the sunshine but the
Night time glow of the moon and
Stars makes me content with those
Big windows.
I would have slept tonight if it
Wasn't for the millions of stars
All competing for my attention.

09/2016

Louisiana Lake
September 2016

SAFE PLACES

Minds should have a safe place
To go and ponder.
A place to ramble through the
Ups and downs of life.
I will hide there in my safe place
While they plot and plan what
Turns they think my life should take.
I must remember that my needs can
Grow in different directions.
I don't want to follow so easily
That I wonder what became of me.
I will just stay here in this warm
Safe place.

09/2015

At Sea
September 14, 2016

PATTERNS

We cannot change the patterns of Life.
We must only observe them
And bend to their will
With Grace,
Living under the careful eyes
Of God.

09/30/2010

Italy
September 30, 2010

MOMENTS

Keeping our hearts and minds open
To the spirit of life.
Stretch the pathways.
Accept that we always have a
Flower yet to open.
Every moment we come upon
is holding a treasure
that we are supposed to find.
Embrace your moments.

01/06/2011

Caribbean Sunrise
January 6, 2011

TOUCHING

Touching is simply another way of
Talking
When you are too tired to talk.
Simply touch me.
I'm here.

01/2011

Blue Moon Over New Mexico
January 2011

PRETTY PACKAGES

We wrap our little seeds of effort,
Desire, passion, and curiosity
In pretty little packages and designs.
In the end it rarely has anything to
Do with the sweetness of what grows
Within us.
Even fruits have to grow within a
Covering that must be peeled away
When ripe to reach the sweetness.
Help me remove the pretty packages
And peel away the covering so we
Can have the sweetness of life set free.

01/2011

Death Valley Sunrise
January 2011

GOD'S TOUCH

Knowing you is such a treasure.
It opens the skies of all time.
It lets the song come out of the seas.
It lets the heart, like a photograph
Being developed, makes a perfect
Picture of what it is like to be
Touched by you.

01/2011

BEING MYSELF

All your love, as big as the sky,
Fills my heart and helps me become
More of myself.
I would do anything for you.
Would you show me yourself?

05/2010

POETRY OF LIFE

I must not only write
The poetry of life
I must start to live the
Poetry of life.
Only in living it can
Others see our soul.

04/2006

West India Coast
April 2006

CRICKETS

Just as the warm sun of summer
Makes a cricket sing,
The quality of bein held
Enlivens the heart.

02/2011

Kentucky sunrise
February 2011

EMERGENCE

*My choice to learn you
And to know you is my
Emergence into living
Over hiding-
Of being over thinking-
Of participating over
Observing-
Of thriving over surviving.*

01/06/2011

Newellton Louisiana
January 6, 2011

ANTICIPATION

Wondering what the future
Might bring?
What's in store for us out there?
Anticipating the fulfillment of
Our hopes and dreams.
That's what life is all about.
Living in the anticipation for a
Future of love, peace, and
Contentment.
For the joy of being together
As one in mind, heart, and Spirit.

11/08/2010

PREREQUISITES

There is no prerequisite for
Finding each other's hearts.
Nothing to prepare for,
Nothing to set up in advance.
Just brush aside what separates
Us
And land in what is before us–
Each other.

11/07/2009

Texas
November 7, 2009

REST

*Rest like a great tree
As praise and blame,
Gain and loss,
Pleasure and sorrow
Go like the wind.
Our blessings come in
Learning when to reach
And hold,
And when to put our
Hands in our pockets.*

01/2011

Pacific at Sea
January 2011

OUR AUTHENTIC PRESENCE

The ways of others will fill the
Space we live in if we don't
Fill that space with our
Own authentic presence.
We have to be aware of who we
Are to keep the ways of others
From sweeping our authenticity
Away.
Be aware of thieves that sneak
In during the night.

11/2005

Oklahoma Sunrise
November 2005

THINKING

No amount of thinking
Can keep you from thinking.

01/2011

Las Vegas
January 2011

JOIN THEM

They say -
If you can't beat 'em
Join them.
So, I ask,
If I become an alcoholic like them,
Get addicted to cigarettes as they are,
Demean you and your name,
As I have heard them do,
Become inconsiderate and
Selfish as their actions show,
Do you think I could win
A life with you?

09/2010

At Sea
July 2010

STRAIGHT AHEAD

Yesterday-
Do you remember how we met?
Today-
Do you remember what I said?
Tomorrow-
Will you remember how I cared?
I have no time for hate
I am hurrying straight ahead.
And although I hurry
I have all the hours left in the
Day to show love.
It would be such a waste if
We don't love freely and straight ahead.

07/2010

South Africa
July 2010

CLOCKS

No wall can stop love.
No clock can bring it back.
Hold on tight!
We must stay prepared
Looking for—
Seeking—
Searching.
Holding on to our love
Before the clock of time
Runs out.

07/2012

San Diego Sunset
June 2010

OUR NEEDS

It is hard to believe that all we
Need is right before us,
Around us, and within us.
Our task is to be rooted and
Patient.
I see your need to gently touch
A yellow petal,
And when you do I see the
Beauty touch you.

08/22/2009

RIVERS AGAIN

We share the same river
It flows beneath us and
Through us,
From one dry heart to
The next.
When shared we lose
Our stubbornness the way
Fists wear open when held
Under the stream of love.

08/2008

West Africa
July 2008

HAVING YOU

If I dare to hear you
I will feel you like the sun
And grow in your direction—
And you in mine.

10/2008

Sri Lanka
October 2008

STAYING WELL

Feeling the sun even in
The dark.
Knowing there is water
Even in the desert.
Knowing there is love
Even when lonely.
Knowing there is peace
Even in the middle of turmoil.
Our wellness lies within
The peace in our hearts.

01/2011

Italy Coast
January 2011

WHO'S TO SAY

Who's to say that the colors of
Passion doesn't line our faces
The instant we grow tired of
Living in the tight cocoon of
Our own making?
Who's to say the journey to love
Doesn't begin the moment we
Give voice to that loneliness that
No one wants to hear?
Every effort that is allowed its
Full beat within, will ripple as a birth.
Enter each day by inviting one
Deep feeling to sprout from you.

11/2011

Angel Cloud
November 2010

MOVING THE STONES

Like the Spanish farmer pushing the
Stones in the river to keep the water
Flowing,
Such is the never-ending work of life
And relationships, the moving of the
Heavy stones between us.
Repositioning of the heavy things that
Get in the way so we can continue.
Stones like not seeing-
Not hearing, or being present.
Not feeling, or risking the truth.
Not risking the hearts need to live out
In the open.
We all need help moving the stones.
will you help me?
If you have stones to move
I will be there.

01/2011

LIFE

Life is not a matter of taste or feel,
But of awakening.
Life is not a matter of finding things
Pleasing, or disturbing, but of things
Completed.
Life is not a matter of liking or disliking,
But instead, it is about the opening
Of the geography of our soul.

01/2011

Mexico
January 2011

AT FIRST SIGHT

The moment of God sight,
Heart site,
Soul site.
It's the seeing of revelations,
The feeling of oneness that
Overcomes us when nothing
Stands in the way.
Certainly, and beautifully,
this happens when we first truly see
each other and fall sweetly into
the miracle of each other's presence.
When I am there in heart site and soul site,
I can truly see you as you are,
through God's site.
I can touch you like you have touched
my heart

01/2014

Laguna Beach California
January 2014

HABITS

We all walk around within the
Numbness of our habits and routines.
So often we take the marvel of
Ordinary life for granted.
What wonderous things might lie out
There in our universe if we can only
Step out of our comfort zones and
Try life.

11/2010

Freeport Bahamas
November 2010

THE EAR

The ear is only a petal that
Grows from the heart.
When we hear each other
It all becomes a garden.

01/2011

Mediterranean Sea
January 2011

SPEAKING

We speak before we speak.
We tip our head like a tree
Leaning, tired of waiting for
The sun. Before we blink, we know
Each other.
We tell our whole story before
We even open our mouths.

01/2014

Blood Moon over Miami
January 2014

HEARTS

We tire ourselves by fighting
what our hearts want to join.
Seldom do we realize that both
Strength and peace comes from
Our hearts beating in unison.

11/2007

Santa Monica
November 2007

CELLS OF THE HEART

Every time we dare to voice
What beats between our hearts
We invite some other cells of
Our hearts to find what lives
Between us.
Without even knowing it there
Exists a common beat between
Our hearts just waiting to be felt.
In unity the cells of our hearts Sing.

11/2009

Philippines
November 2009

TO JOURNEY

To journey without being changed
Is to be a nomad.
To change without journeying
Is to become inconstant.
To journey and be transformed
By the experience is to be a Pilgrim.

10/2008

Texas Sunrise
October 2008

OBSTACLES

There are many obstacles' that
Prevents experiencing the fullness
Of life.
Hesitancy keeps us away from
Many experiences.
Doubt keeps us from accepting
Some of the pleasures of life.
Fear prevents our being fully
Content with each other.
Removing the obstacles is our key
To true happiness.

10/2008

Lenticular Cloud over Dublin, Ireland
October 2008

www.ingramcontent.com/pod-product-compliance
Lightning Source LLC
LaVergne TN
LVHW061625070526
838199LV00070B/6584